SHOUT

Celebrating God and His Victory

SHOUT

Celebrating God and His Victory

Billy Gibson

Copyright © 2006 by Billy Gibson

Book Design by Keith Crabtree / crabtreedesign.com
Production by BlankPageCreative.com

All rights reserved. This book is protected under the copyright law of the United States of America. This book may not be copied or reprinted for commercial gain or profit. The use of short quotations or occasional page copying for personal or group study is permitted and encouraged. Permission will be granted upon request.

All Scripture quotations, unless otherwise indicated, are taken from the New King James Version and the New Living Translation.

Printed in the United States of America
Published by Billy Gibson Ministries, Inc.

ISBN-10: 1-56394-999-7

DEDICATION

I dedicate this book to the churches and the individuals who believed in the message of *"SHOUT."* Your prayers and financial contributions made this book a reality. I pray great blessing on you for your generous investment!

CONTENTS

INTRODUCTION   9

SECTION ONE: SHOUT TO IT
Chapter 1   Shouting Brings the Prodigal Home   13
Chapter 2   Shouting Brings the Walls Down   21
Chapter 3   Shouting is a Mighty Weapon   27
Chapter 4   Shouting Brings Change   33

SECTION TWO: SHOUT OVER THE ENEMY AND THE MOUNTAINS YOU FACE
Chapter 5   Shouting Brings Victory   41
Chapter 6   Shouting Brings Miracles   49
Chapter 7   Shouting is Celebrating   55
Chapter 8   Shouting Brings Healing   61

SECTION THREE: SHOUT INTO HIS PRESENCE
Chapter 9   Shouting is Praise   69
Chapter 10   Shouting in Faith   75

SECTION FOUR: A PROGRESSIVE SHOUT
Chapter 11   Shouting is Crying Out   87
Chapter 12   Shouting Defeats the Giant   93

SECTION FIVE: WHAT TO DO AFTER THE VICTORY
Chapter 13   Shouting is Everlasting   103

INTRODUCTION

My youngest son began to run from God during his senior year in high school. As the months and years passed by, he drifted farther and farther from the Lord and from me. He got involved with drugs and he started doing things I never dreamed he would do. I prayed. I fasted. I exhausted all of my resources, trying to reach him, but nothing seemed to work.

I was ministering in Toronto, Canada, on Easter Sunday night, when the Lord said concerning my son, "Shout to it." Three weeks after I began to shout to the Lord over my son, God answered my prayer and brought healing and restoration. My son has been living for the Lord ever since.

Several months later, after seeing all the healings and miracles that were taking place in the lives of those that had activated this now word, God spoke to me to write this book.

My prayer is that as you shout to the Lord, His victory will be yours!

SECTION ONE

Shout To It

*Oh, clap your hands, all you peoples!
Shout to God with the voice of triumph!
Psalm 47:1*

Chapter 1

Shouting Brings the Prodigal Home

God tells us something very important about Himself in Isaiah 55:8-9, "For My thoughts are not your thoughts, nor are your ways My ways, says the Lord. For as the heavens are higher than the earth, so are My ways higher than your ways, and My thoughts than your thoughts."

God's thinking and His ways are so much higher than ours. What God is telling us in this scripture is that He does not think like you and I do. His ways are different from ours.

God's ways may not always seem logical. At times in your walk with God, you may have to get your heart above your head. Proverbs 3:5-6 says it this way, "Trust in the Lord with all your heart, and lean not on your own understanding; in all your ways acknowledge Him, and He shall direct your paths." God may ask us to do something that causes us to go beyond our intellect, our inhibitions, and our limitations, in order to stretch us into new dimensions. The Bible says in 2 Corinthians 5:7, "We walk by faith and not by sight." We need to stop being moved by what we see and start being moved by what we know, which is the Word of God.

The Bible is full of instances in which God does things that do not seem logical. For example, a story is recorded in the fifth chapter of 2 Kings, concerning a man named Naaman. This man was a commander of the Syrian army, and he was a leper. Naaman had a servant, a young Israelite maiden that had been captured in a war. When the girl heard Naaman had leprosy, she said, "Oh that my master would go to the prophet in Israel and be healed." So Naaman went to the king and told him what the Israelite girl had said.

Then the king of Syria wrote to the king of Israel saying, "I am sending my commander to you to be healed."

When the king of Israel read the letter he tore his clothes and said, "Am I God that I can heal?"

But Elisha, the prophet of God, hearing what had happened sent word to the king, "Send Naaman to me."

So Naaman went to Elisha's house. When he got there, Elisha did not even come out to meet him. He just gave his servant a message for Naaman, "Go to the Jordan River and dip in it seven times and you will be healed." Now, I do not know what you might think of these instructions, but to me they do not seem logical. Imagine going into your doctor's office one morning and saying, "Doctor, I have leprosy." Then the doctor looks at you and says, "I have just the medicine you need. There's a little pond out back. If you go out there and dip in it seven times, you will be healed." You would probably walk away saying, "That guy is a quack."

Naaman was furious. He told those who traveled with him, "At least he could have picked a cleaner river." But one of his associates said to him, "If he had asked you to do something difficult, would you not have done it?" So he finally obeyed the word of the Lord, even though it seemed ridiculous, even though it was probably embarrassing. He went into the Jordan River and dipped seven times. When he came up the seventh time, the Bible said his skin was like a baby's skin.

In Mark, the eighth chapter, another story is recorded that shows God does not always act in the way we assume He will. A blind man was brought to Jesus for healing and Jesus spit in his eye. Can you imagine going to the doctor's office and saying, "I'm blind. I need your help." And then you hear a spitting sound. "Hey, Doc," I'm sure we would say, "Don't be spitting on me." Do you understand what I am saying? Jesus acted in a way that did not seem logical. And yet the Bible says in verse 23, "The Lord healed him."

I have two sons, Lance and Jared. Both my boys play sports and they are especially good in basketball. Lance, the oldest, attended college on a full athletic scholarship and Jared, the youngest, was following in the footsteps of his older brother.

In August, 2000, between Jared's junior and senior year in high school, he attended a youth camp where I was speaking. At the end of the week, Jared told me he felt God was calling him into the ministry. It was an exciting time in the life of my family. It seemed things could not get any better than they were in those summer months before Jared would begin his last year in high school. Then something happened.

A few months into his senior year, things began to change in Jared's life. For the first time he had problems in his studies. The school district's policy required that athletes maintain at least a "C" in every subject to be eligible to play sports. Poor grades in math lost Jared his eligibility to play basketball for part of the season. His life had been basketball. From a young boy he honed his skills, consistently leading his team in scoring. A team leader and a player's player, my son loved basketball. His one goal was to play college ball at a major university. But with the loss of part of the season's eligibility, came the loss of his dream. When he did not receive a scholarship, his hope was shattered and he lost his motivation for life. Jared started on a downward spiral, a journey into darkness.

Jared not only severed his relationship with God, he also cut me out of his life. Sin began to control his actions. Drugs, alcohol, things a parent would never dream could happen to their child, became a constant to him. I knew the devil was trying to kill my son. My heart was breaking. This boy, my youngest son, who had told me, "Dad, I feel like God is calling me into the ministry," was someone I could not even recognize.

While ministering in South Texas, I remember being awakened one morning in a hotel room with news that Jared had been in a terrible car accident. Driving 85 miles an hour, he fell asleep at the wheel and crashed head on into a tree. Yet, he walked away from it. I knew this had to be his wake-up call. Surely he would get his life straight now. But it didn't faze him. He acted as though it was no big deal, and when I tried to talk with him, he let me know he did not believe in the God I believed in anymore.

My relationship with Jared fractured, as though he had slammed a door in my face. Grief began to build inside me. Whenever I talked with him on the phone, the conversation was like talking with a dead man. There was no expression in his voice. This brilliant young man, with ambition and a promising future, had now dropped out of community college, and could not keep a job. Depression controlled his life. His thoughts and attitudes reflected darkness and death, even in the books he read. As I watched him descend into this abyss, I began to carry his pain of shame. The more I prayed, the more the Lord allowed me to feel his hidden pain, to suffer the shame Satan had bound around Jared's heart.

This did not go on for a few weeks or even a few months. This went on for three years. I fasted. I prayed. I can't tell you how many times I cried myself to sleep over my son. Satan relentlessly came at my mind with the fiery darts of condemnation, "What kind of father are you? How can you pray for other people's children when you cannot even have the faith for your own?" A continuous battle raged in my soul.

One Easter Sunday night, I was preaching in Toronto, Canada. At the close of the service, after ministering to those wanting prayer, I was walking around in the front of the church, praising God while worship music played in the background. Then I heard God speak three words to me, "Shout to it." I knew immediately what He was saying. Shout to Jared's release.

"Lord," I said, "this doesn't seem logical. I've fasted and prayed, and nothing has happened. But I'm desperate. If You want me to shout to Jared's release, I'll do it."

Then I heard the voice of the Lord deep inside me, "Billy, I don't want you to shout at the enemy. I don't want you to shout out of fear. I don't want you to shout out of desperation. I want you to shout with joy and with a voice of triumph to Me over your son." I began to shout over Jared day and night.

One week passed ... nothing. Two weeks passed ... still nothing. It is difficult to shout for joy when you see no change in your circumstances. It is easy to shout after the healing, or the victory, or when the prodigal son comes home. There is no problem being excited then, but what about when the picture does not change?

And yet, God said, "I want you to shout to it." And because God said it, I did it! I continued shouting to the Lord. I told no one of God's instruction to me, but I became consumed with this word. All my available time was spent studying what God had to say in the Bible about shouting. Every time I got a new revelation, and every time I began to shout to God for my son's release, a sense of expectancy would rise up in my spirit.

Two more weeks went by and still no word from Jared. I continued to shout to the Lord with joy and with a voice of triumph.

Then one morning my phone rang, "Hey Dad, what's

going on?"

"Lance, how are you?"

"Dad, this isn't Lance, it's Jared!"

"Jared?" I did not even recognize him. There was so much life in his voice.

"Yeah, Dad, it's me. I called to see if you would pray for me."

Remember, we are talking about a guy that a year ago told me he did not even believe in the God I believed in anymore. We are talking about a guy that did not want anything to do with God, or church, or me. And he was asking me to pray for him.

"Dad, I just came back from my second interview with Daystar Television. They want to hire and train me to be a graphic artist. They'll let me know for sure within ten days if I get the job. Dad, I really want this job. Will you pray I get it?"

Knowing exactly what that father felt when he looked up and saw his prodigal running toward home, I humbly answered, "Yes, son, I'll pray for you. Let's pray right now."

"Dad," he said, "I've already made things right with God, now I need to make them right with you. Would you forgive me?"

When I hung up the phone, in between the shouts, I said, "Lord, please expedite this request."

One hour later, Jared called and said, "Dad, I got the job!"

For over a year, Jared has been working at a Christian television station, hearing the Word of God every day. God has restored our relationship and brought life back into my son.

Let me tell you something I have learned. When God says to do something, just do it! Do not worry about what everyone else will think. It is amazing to me that we worry what people think about the way we worship God. Sometimes we will not shout or praise Him because we are concerned with how we look to others. Just remember, when all is said and done, they are not the audience. He is.

Through my time of ministering to God for my son, I became consumed with this truth of the shout. I was driving down the road one day and the Lord said, "I want you to preach on this."

And I remember saying, "Preach on it? How do you preach on shout? Do you just get up and tell everybody to shout?" I did not know. But as I listened to God, He gave me a message for the church. He told me to share it everywhere I go. And I have. I am amazed by all the miracles and unusual things that are happening because of the obedience to this now word. The message of *"SHOUT"* is changing people's lives and setting them free.

Chapter 2

Shouting Brings the Walls Down

As I have continued to study scriptures, concerning the shout, God has begun to give me a new understanding of familiar passages. I have read these verses countless times, ministered, using them as texts, but never had the revelation I have now.

For instance, the scriptures recorded in the sixth chapter of Joshua. Verse 1 says, "Now Jericho was securely shut up because of the children of Israel. None went out and none came in." Israel, God's chosen people, had been wandering in the wilderness for forty years and now it was time to enter into Canaan, which is known as the Promised Land. In order to gain access to their inheritance, the Israelites must pass through Jericho. And what had the enemy done? He built up these big walls, hindering their entrance.

It is the same today. The enemy has built up walls

surrounding your promise, and he is telling you, "You cannot come in and your promise cannot come out." We develop a mind set based on what we see and begin to believe the situation will never change. That person will never be saved; that healing will never come; that miracle will never happen. When we look toward our promise, all we see are mighty walls. We know it is a promise from God because the Bible says in 2 Corinthians 1:20, "All the promises of God in Jesus are yes and amen." Not just yes, but yes and *amen*, meaning yes and *so be it*. We know this. And yet, we see our promise surrounded by these mighty walls the enemy has built to keep us out.

But I love verse 2 in Joshua 6. "And the Lord said to Joshua: 'See! I have given Jericho into your hand, its king, and the mighty men of valor.'" The verse begins with God speaking to Joshua. "And the Lord said." Remember, God will always speak to you when you face impossibility. "And the Lord said to Joshua: 'See!'" The word s*ee* is important in this text. It means to *envision*. It means to *foresee*. God is saying, "Joshua, before the wall ever comes down; before that king and those people are ever defeated; I want you to see I have already given them to you. I have given them into your hand." If something is given into my hand that means I now possess it. He told Joshua it did not matter what he saw in the natural. He had already given Jericho into his hand.

You must change the way you see things. You must see your healing. You must see your miracle. You must see your lost loved ones saved. I often ask people if they have loved ones who are lost. Invariably, their response is,

"Yes." My goal is to help those people see their loved ones saved, regardless of the circumstances. Rather than seeing a mighty wall, God wants us to see His mighty power.

God then told Joshua He had not only given the city into his hands, but also its *king*, which represents *authority*, and its *mighty men of valor*, which speaks of *power*. That is important. Do you know what God was saying? He was not only giving Joshua the city, but also its authority and its power. There was about to be a power and authority change in Jericho.

When there is a power and authority change in that lost loved one's life, they will come to God. Those walls will be knocked down. Satan will not rule over their life anymore. There is going to be a new king in their life, a new power of the Spirit. The walls will be a thing of the past.

God's instructions to Joshua became more amazing, "Here is what I want you to do. I want you to march around the city once every day for six days. But on the seventh day, I want you to march around the city seven times." God told Joshua to march around the city seven times with seven priests, blowing seven trumpets, or in the Hebrew, shofars. When the sound of the shofar was released, it would frighten the enemy because it literally represented the breath of God. And then He said, "When those priests sound that long blast, I want all the people to shout with a great shout."

The instructions God gave Joshua did not seem logical, but Joshua followed them anyway. Many times God will speak something to us and then we begin questioning it. We try to reason it out. But we'll never understand some commands until we obey them first. Obedience unlocks understanding and blessing. If we want God's results, we have to do things God's way.

What if I had argued with the Lord in Toronto? When the Lord said to shout to it, what if I had answered, "Come on, Lord, that's a little embarrassing. What do you mean, shout?"

I was raised in a large family, nine children – six boys, three girls. That is eleven people in a small three-bedroom house. When the show *Survivor* came on television, I really related, but they had nothing on us. It was survival every day at our house. Six boys in one room – you figure that one out. My friends would come over to my house, walk in my room, and ask, "Where's your bed?" I would tell them, "You're standing on it." I thought everyone slept on the floor. I did not know any better.

But it did not matter how difficult a situation looked, my mother would never allow a bad attitude. She had an attitude adjuster. And if we even looked like we were going to have a bad attitude or try to get smart with her, she would start reaching for that adjuster. I cannot tell you how many times just that reach would change my whole attitude. I went from lousy to, "Okay, Mama, whatever you say. Put it down, Mama." She would never allow us to question her.

But when God tells us to do something, we question Him. "Why God?" We start whining and complaining when all God wants is a simple "Yes, Sir."

Joshua obeyed God and the Israelites took their promise with a shout! Over and over in the Word, God tells us to shout to our victory. Shout to the Lord! I wonder why it feels so strange, and even uncomfortable in our society. Have you noticed it is not uncomfortable to shout at ball games? We do not walk away from events like that thinking how crazy the people acted over their favorite teams. But take some of those same people and place them inside the walls of a church, and the most incredible thing happens. They lose their ability to shout to the Lord for the promises He has given them. If only they realized that just like the children of Israel, their release many times will come in the shout.

God wants the message out! He wants us to understand the power of the shout.

Chapter 3

Shouting is a Mighty Weapon

Obedience unlocks understanding and blessing. That is why the Bible says in Isaiah 1:19, "If you're willing and obedient, you will eat the good of the land." There are many ways to be willing and obedient, and shouting is one of those ways.

Shouting means several things in the Hebrew and in the Greek. It means to *shout for joy*. It means to *lift your voice*. Whenever you read in the Bible that people are lifting their voice, it means they are shouting. Shouting means *noise*. It means to *cry out*. Whenever you read that the people cried out, it literally means they shouted. In fact, more modern translations will interpret it as shout rather than cry out. Shouting means to *cry out in distress*; it also means *a war cry*. When armies faced each other, they would release shouts. Later in this book, we will look at the reasons the shout was released as a war cry, and the results that occurred with these mighty shouts.

The word for shout is sometimes translated *alarm*. When you read in Joel the second chapter, the prophetic scriptures concerning the second return of the Lord, He said, "Sound the alarm on My holy mountain." He is literally saying, sound the shout.

Some people may not like the idea of shouting, but they shouted when they entered this world. The first thing they did was cry out. God obviously planned that each individual He created would release one hearty shout during his lifetime. Does He have a sense of humor or what?

Shouting is praise to God. There are seven Hebrew words that define praise. Anywhere you see the word *praise* in the Old Testament, it derives from one of these seven words. One of these seven words is *shabach*, and it means to *shout*. This confirms that shouting is praise to God. Praise is very important. Because Psalm 149:6-9 says, "Let the high praises of God be in their mouth, and a two-edged sword in their hand, to execute vengeance on the nations, and punishments on the people; to bind their kings with chains, and their nobles with fetters of irons, to execute on them the written judgment. This honor have all His saints."

Do you see that? It is an honor to praise God. We do not praise Him because we have nothing else to do. We praise God because it is a key to getting into His presence. If you want to get in my car, and the door is locked, you need a key. Yelling at it will accomplish nothing. Being friends with me will not get you in that car. You have to have the right key for the right door. The wrong key will never open a locked door, and no key will have the same results.

Shouting is a mighty weapon for every believer. 2 Corinthians 10:3-4 says this, "For though we walk in the flesh, we do not war according to the flesh. For the weapons of our warfare are not carnal but mighty in God for pulling down strongholds." Praise is a mighty weapon that will pull strongholds down. And it is a key.

In Revelation 3:7, Jesus said that He held the key of David in His hand. If you look at the life of King David, you will find that he was a praiser and a worshiper.

Some people misunderstand the shout. So let me tell you what it is not. Shouting is not yelling at God. It is not lifting your voice because God has a hearing problem. The true essence of what shouting is, and the reason that we shout, is wrapped up in this truth: *Shouting is celebrating our God and His victory.* If you go to a ball game, and you hear all the fans shouting, their team must be winning. But when their team is losing 40 to zero, you will not hear them shouting. In fact, they will get really quiet. But turn that game around, and an explosion of noise occurs.

You would think the church would pick up on this. We win! God woke me up just a few weeks ago and said, "Tell my people that when they shout to me, I will move on their behalf."

There was a man in Wake Forest, North Carolina, who heard this message on a Sunday morning. The next day his five-year-old daughter woke up with a 104-degree fever. While traveling to work, he decided to put the truth he had learned into practice. He began to shout and celebrate God's victory in her healing. He shouted all the way to his place of employment, a one-hour drive. He told

SHOUT Celebrating God and His Victory

me, "When I got there, I called my wife. She said the fever had broken, and my daughter was outside playing."

Praise accompanies victory and victory accompanies praise. After Solomon left the throne, Israel split into two kingdoms. One part of the kingdom kept the name Israel, but they did not keep God's law. The other part of the territory became Judah. The word *Judah* literally means *praise*. 2 Chronicles 13 tells the story of a battle between the two, and verse 13 says, "But Jeroboam (the wicked king of Israel) caused an ambush to go around behind them; so they were in front of Judah, and the ambush was behind them." The enemy was attempting to wipe out praise, by annihilating the tribe of Judah. If he could get rid of the praisers, the people would not have been able to get into God's presence. And without God's presence, they would have been defeated. If you do not praise God, you do not go into His presence. If you do not go into His presence, you are dead. That is why a person can walk into any church, and if the presence of God is not there, even people who do not know God will say, "Man, that service was dead."

If you do not stay in God's presence, you might not be dead physically, but you will certainly be dead spiritually. And walking into a church building is not a guarantee that He is present in your life. Psalm 100:4 says, "Enter His gates with thanksgiving, come into His courts with praise." Thanksgiving and praise are the keys to getting into God's presence and they are available to every believer. The question has never been, "Do you have those keys?" The question has always been, "Are you willing to use them?" The question has never been, "Can I praise God?"

The question has always been, "Will I praise God?"

Jeroboam, king of Israel, is attempting to knock out Judah. Remember, *Judah* means *praise*. Verse 14 says, "And when Judah looked around, to their surprise the battle line was at both front and rear; and they cried out to the Lord, and the priests sounded the trumpets." Judah was surrounded. Everywhere they looked they saw the enemy. They were being attacked from both ends.

Verse 15, "Then the men of Judah gave a shout; and as the men of Judah shouted, it happened that God struck Jeroboam (Israel's king) and all Israel before Abijah (Judah's king) and Judah. And the children of Israel fled before Judah, and God delivered them into their hand." As the men of Judah shouted, it happened that God struck Jeroboam and Israel and they turned and ran. Then God delivered them into the hands of the praisers. Praise is a powerful weapon.

At the close of a service I was conducting in Oklahoma City, an 81-year-old man came down that had just been released from the hospital. His doctor had told him that his heart was weak and his body was worn out. He was very feeble. He had no strength or energy. Even using his walker, he needed the help of two men to get to the front of the church. He was that frail.

When he got to the altar, this man began to release a shout to the Lord. I prayed over him, shouting to God for his health, and then went on to pray for others. A remarkable thing happened. When this elderly man left the church, he was carrying his walker over the top of his head. And instead of shuffling weakly up the isle, he marched out of the church, completely healed. During this revival, he never missed a service. Each night he would grab me in a bear hug, and declare, "I'm getting stronger every day." When you shout to the Lord, He is going to move on your behalf.

In Mark 10:46-48, Jesus traveled to Jericho with His disciples. "And as He went out of Jericho with His disciples and a great multitude, blind Bartimaeus, the son of Timaeus, sat by the road begging. And when he heard that it was Jesus of Nazareth, he began to cry out and say, 'Jesus, Son of David, have mercy on me!' Then many warned him to be quiet."

Crying out or shouting out to God may embarrass the people around you. They may even attempt to quiet you. But you have to get louder than the doubters. The Bible says Bartimaeus began to shout out even more. "Son of David have mercy on me!" Verse 49 says, "So Jesus stood still." And you know the rest of the story. He called for Bartimaeus and he threw off his coat and ran. The Romans had a law that if you were blind, you were to wear a particular garment, signifying your blindness. Failure to wear it resulted in death.

Bartimaeus made a bold statement when he threw off that coat. He was leaving the life of a blind man behind. And Jesus healed him! Many people wanted Jesus' attention that day, but Bartimaeus shouted out and God heard him. God hears our cries.

Chapter 4

Shouting Brings Change

My wife and I were recently in the city of Burleson, Texas. At the end of the service when I asked for people who wanted prayer to come forward, a young woman came hurrying to the front, tears streaming down her face. Immediately, we went to her and prayed for her salvation. After the service she told us her story.

"I've been a stripper most of my adult life, but I'm not going to live like that anymore. God truly saved me tonight. My problem is I have no education. I have no training. I don't know what kind of a job I can get. When I quit this lifestyle, I won't have a place to stay or income to find another place. But I'm not going back. Will you pray for me?"

We began to shout to the Lord with praise and a voice of triumph that the victory Jesus had paid for would be manifested in the life of this woman. Then the Spirit of the Lord impressed me, and I began to pray prophetically over her. I told her God would turn her life completely around in the next 24 hours.

The next morning this woman had to go to court and stand before a judge for several outstanding parking tickets she had ignored and not paid. The judge looked at her background, at the lifestyle she had been living, and was not impressed. "This does not sit well with me, Young Lady."

In a repentant voice she asked for mercy. "Judge, I know I have done wrong, but I don't live that way anymore. Last night I went to church and gave my heart to Jesus. I promise I am never going back to that kind of life." Something in her touched something in that judge. "I am going to dismiss the charges against you, Young Lady. All you need to pay is the twenty-dollar court cost."

"Thank you, sir. But Judge, I don't even have twenty dollars."

The judge then took a remarkable action. Hitting his gavel, he told the waiting defendants, "We're taking a short recess. Young Lady, come back into my chambers." When she went into his office, he pulled out a twenty-dollar bill and gave it to her. He told her not to tell anyone and to "keep living for Jesus."

By the end of the day, she had another place to stay, she had money, and she had a new job. Within 24 hours God totally changed everything in her life. God hears our cries.

Numbers 23:21 records a story of a prophet named Balaam, who was hired by an enemy of Israel to prophesy against God's people. But he could not do it. In fact, as he attempted to speak, a prophetic word came from him, foreseeing the coming of the Lord Jesus. "The shout of a king is among them," he said. It is amazing that the prophet Balaam mentioned shouting in conjunction with the coming Messiah.

Did you know God shouts? In Isaiah 42:13 it says, "The Lord shall go forth like a mighty man; He shall stir up His zeal like a man of war. He shall cry out, yes, shout aloud; He shall prevail against His enemies." All through the Bible you read where it says, "Great is the Lord and greatly to be praised." The word *great* in that verse means *loud*. It could be translated, "Loud is the Lord, and loudly to be praised!"

You may hear some say, "I don't know about all this shouting. I'm not sure I like it." Well, if you do not like shouting, you are going to have a big problem in heaven, because they are shouting there. Not only does God shout, but angels do also. Revelation 5:11, "Then I looked, and I heard the voice of many angels around the throne, the living creatures, and the elders; and the number of them was ten thousand times ten thousand and thousands of thousands, saying with a loud voice: 'Worthy is the Lamb who was slain to receive power and riches and wisdom, and strength and honor and glory and blessing!'" Thousands upon thousands are shouting to God.

Another depiction of heaven is recorded in Revelation 7:9, "After these things I looked, and behold, a great multitude which no one could number, of all nations, tribes, peoples, and tongues, standing before the throne and before the Lamb, clothed in white robes, with palm branches in their hands, and crying out with a loud voice, saying, 'Salvation belongs to our God who sits on the throne, and to the Lamb!'"

Did you know when Jesus returns He will come with a shout? 1Thessalonians 4:16 says, "For the Lord Himself will descend from heaven with a shout." I believe God likes shouting.

Shouting always accompanies victory and celebration. People shout at ball games because they are winning. They are expressing themselves. They are emotional. They are happy.

Psalm 66:1 says, "Shout joyfully praises to God all the earth." Verse 4 says, "Everything on the earth will worship You, they will sing Your praises, shouting Your name, and glorious songs."

Shouting is not a new concept. In the '60s, many of you were singing and dancing to a song encouraging you to *"Twist and Shout."* In the '70s, some of you were celebrating to a song that went something like this, *"You know you make me want to shout."* In 1983, Motley Crue, a secular group, came out with a title song for an album, *"Shout to the Devil."* When interviewed by reporters of their intentions, they were quick to say, "We were just having fun and kidding around. We didn't mean anything spiritual by it."

But in 1993, just ten years after Motley Crue attempted to get the world shouting to the devil, the all-time greatest worship song ever written, came from a young woman by the name of Darlene Zschech. It was entitled *"Shout to the Lord."* Even now, many years later, on any given Sunday all over the world, between 25 and 30 million people sing this song. The miracle of this story is that the majority of that 25 to 30 million people belong to denominations that don't even believe in shouting. If you were to shout in their church, they would probably kick you out. And they're singing *"Shout to the Lord"* every Sunday morning. God certainly has a sense of humor.

While ministering in Allentown, Pennsylvania, I met a man who had been suffering from asthma almost his entire life. On inhalers and steroids, he had never been able to take a deep breath. He began to shout to the Lord Sunday morning, continuing Sunday evening, then Monday and Tuesday. He did not ask God for anything, but just continued to shout to the Lord. He came to me on Tuesday night and said, "This morning, for the first time in my life that I can ever remember, I took a deep breath." He continued, "I'm no longer on inhalers or any steroids." God has healed me of asthma.

Shouting to the Lord brings change.

SECTION TWO

Shout Over The Enemy And The Mountains You Face

*I tell you the truth,
you can say to this mountain,
"May you be lifted up
and thrown into the sea,"
and it will happen.
Mark 11:23*

Chapter 5

Shouting Brings Victory

In 1 Samuel 17, Israel was at war against the Philistines. A battle line had been drawn and every morning each army would go out to the battlefield and line up against one another. The Philistines had a warrior named Goliath in their army. He was a giant! History says he was about 9'9", and weighed 800 to 900 pounds. Every day Goliath would stand and challenge Israel, taunting them with their weaknesses. This went on for forty days. What is interesting about forty days is that the number *forty* is the number for *transition*. Change was coming, and it would not be in the best interest of the enemies of God.

But Goliath, in his pride, didn't have a clue what the God of Israel was up to. Every morning, this brazen giant would stand in front of the army of the Philistines and berate God's people. "Send a man to fight me," he would challenge them. And of course, none would go because all of Israel was dreadfully afraid. They were terrified, from the king on down.

The enemy will always attempt to strike fear into God's people, based on what they see, by having them focus on the problem instead of the answer. Remember what God told Joshua when he was looking at the wall that stood between him and his promise? The first word He spoke to Joshua was *"See!"* Envision. Foresee. "See! I have given Jericho into your hand." You must look at the Lord, and not at the problem. Hebrews 12:2 says, "Looking unto Jesus, the author and finisher of our faith." So many times people come for prayer and they are consumed with the sickness, or the problem, or the lie of the enemy. But our healing, our miracle, comes when we stop focusing on the problem and begin looking to the Lord. We have to recognize that God has already given us the promise because He finishes, or completes, what our faith reaches out for. All the promises of God in Him are yes and amen or *so be it*.

When the army of Israel looked out over the battlefield each morning, all they saw was the magnitude of the enemy. Goliath was huge! Because of his size and his reputation as a skilled warrior, he struck terror in the hearts of the soldiers.

David was a shepherd boy whose older brothers had gone to battle against the Philistines. One morning Jesse, his father, called him in from the field and instructed him to take food to his brothers at the battle front. The Bible says in 1 Samuel 17:20, "So David rose early in the morning, left the sheep with the keeper and took the things and went as Jesse had commanded him."

Traditionally, when armies faced each other in battle, they would begin to shout. As David approached the camp, he heard the army of Israel shouting as they went to confront the enemy on the battlefield. Why would an army shout with such exuberance before a battle? They did it because shouting released adrenalin. It released faith in their ability to win. The enemy hates to hear an army's victory shout. It weakens his ability to win. Remember, *shouting is celebrating our God and His victory.*

David came upon an interesting scene. The army was shouting before their enemy, even though they were afraid, and had no champion to challenge Goliath. But God heard their shout and, as a result, sent David to defeat the giant.

When David heard the challenge coming from the mountain of the enemy, his question was immediate, "Who is this uncircumcised Philistine, that he should defy the armies of the living God?" I can almost hear those close enough to hear the question gasp. They looked at that skinny shepherd boy, someone who had never even fought in a single battle, and probably laughed. But they were looking at David, not at the God standing behind him. They were looking at the outward appearance of the shepherd, but God was looking on the heart of a man who understood the enemy had no right to defy the armies of the living God!

How many times have we tried looking at our situation logically, rather than looking to God who has all power over any circumstance? God does not always do things that seem logical. He certainly did not that day.

God picked a shepherd boy with a slingshot as

a weapon to go against a giant, with an armor bearer protecting him with a huge shield, a spear with a 166-pound spearhead, and armor covering his entire body. After getting King Saul to go along with his plan, David goes down to a brook, and picked up five small smooth stones. Who would ever think that a slingshot and a stone would work against all the armor of the enemy? But even a giant has to see, so there was a small opening in his armor. Bam! The stone hit Goliath right between the eyes and he fell to the ground.

I always wondered why David picked up five stones. Was he keeping a supply, in case God missed on the first attempt? No way. Did you know that Goliath had four brothers? David was ready to take on the whole bunch. Israel said, "He's too big to fight." David said, "He's too big to miss."

Your inner picture is the key. The way you look at a circumstance creates your paradigm. Each man in Israel's army looked at Goliath, compared him to himself and felt small. David looked at the giant, compared him to his God and knew who the small one was!

We hear the word cancer and great fear envelopes us. It becomes a giant of horror in our lives. But when you take cancer, and put it next to God, guess who the small one is?

We look at our lost loved one and get a mind set that this is as good as it will ever be. But when you take them, and put them next to God, guess who the small one is?

Do you know what is so amazing about this story? The army shouted and God brought the answer. And He brought it through the most unlikely person. God's ways are not our ways. Can you imagine choosing David, a shepherd boy, to fight against Goliath? Can you see King Saul lining up his army, looking them over, going past all his experienced warriors, and saying, "Well, nobody is good enough here to go against the giant. Let's see, why don't I get this young shepherd boy to go kill Goliath?" No, we all know that would not have happened, but God chose David. Sometimes God will use the most unlikely source to be the answer for your situation. Our challenge is that we ask God to help us, and we have a mind set as to how He will accomplish the task. We pray, and when God attempts to answer outside our realm of understanding, we miss it. And then we wonder why God never answers our prayers.

When my son, Jared, left the familiar of God's protection and became a prodigal, my heart was broken. Death was written all over him. I had nightmares, and was tormented day and night. Even though I prayed and fasted, there was no change in Jared. He kept getting farther and farther away from God. But then God told me to shout in victory over my son.

When I began to shout, I had no clue how God was going to help Jared. I had exhausted every resource I could imagine to reach him and nothing seemed to work. But God said, "Shout to it", so I did. Never in a million years would I have figured out the source God would use to bring my son home. Not one time did I say, "Okay, God, here is how I want You to do this. Have a Christian television station call my son, who is not even living for you, and have them hire him, and then train him, for a position in which he has no experience. Yeah, God, I think that might work." I could have never come up with such a perfect plan.

So many times we put God in a box by saying, "God, here is how I want You to answer my prayer." And many times, because He wants to use the most unlikely source, he brings a David, an answer we would not have been able to come up with.

Remember, the army of God was shouting as they went to face the enemy, even in their fear, they shouted. And God heard them, and used David to defeat the giant. Verse 52 says, "Now the men of Israel and Judah arose and shouted, and pursued the Philistines." The battle began with a shout of victory, and it ended with a shout of victory. The greater the shout ... the greater the victory! The greater the victory ... the greater the shout!

I was in Mesquite, Texas, this past year. A couple in the church where I was ministering had been grieving for three or four weeks because a representative from the State of Texas had come to their house and taken two foster children from them. This Godly couple, both with good jobs, had raised these children from the time they were infants. They had been the only parents these beautiful babies had known for eighteen months. But the biological parents, who were ungodly people, decided they wanted the children back and the state had no alternative but to take them from this couple. The state told them that even if the birth parents decided not to keep the children, they would be returned to the social system of Texas. There was no guarantee this couple would ever get the children back even if that happened. They were told, "You will probably never see these children again. The best thing you can do for yourselves is to forget them." They did not want to forget them. They had been raising them. They loved them. They wanted to adopt these children even though they were told that it would never happen.

Sunday morning I ministered on shouting to the Lord. After hearing the message, this lady told her husband, "Tonight, at the end of the service, we are going to ask Billy to shout with us over the babies."

So they came to the altar weeping uncontrollably and told me their story. "We love those children. We want to adopt them. We believe God gave them to us, and now the State of Texas has taken them away." They continued, "We have been told, we will never see them again. The social workers said our chance of ever getting them back is slim to none. We want to pray for a miracle."

We began shouting together over those children, and for God's will to be done. I left and began to pray with other people. I was told later that the husband shouted so loud and long he lost his voice. This was Sunday night. The following Tuesday morning, there was a knock on the door of this couple's home. Upon opening, they found a social worker from the State of Texas standing there, holding the two children. The two children were then handed over to them. The social worker could not explain why the biological parents had just suddenly given up the children.

But there is more to this story. Because the children had biological parents, it seemed impossible for them to ever be adopted. But seven months after the parents heart-wrenching shout to God, they received a phone call. "We do not understand this, but the biological parents have given up all their rights to these children. If you want, you can adopt them."

Anyone can shout when everything is going great. Anyone can shout after the answer comes. That is the easy part. But what about while you are looking at the problem, while you are facing the enemy? It is important to shout to God with a voice of triumph, while facing the mountain the enemy has placed in front of you, because shouting produces faith.

Chapter 6

Shouting Brings Miracles

2 Chronicles 20 relates one of my favorite stories in the Bible. The first verse begins, "It happened after this." It is important to understand what the writer was referring to, so we have to look back at what occurred in the nineteenth chapter. A man named Jehoshaphat had become the king of Judah at the death of his father and began to reform Judah. He directed the people to follow God's commandments again. This angered the enemy of God.

Whenever we begin to do what is right, Satan will come and attempt to stop us. This is a critical period in our faith. We must not stop. It is during this period that God is working to bring our victory. Because Jehoshaphat began teaching the people what was right in God's eyes, the enemy was stirred up. The scripture goes on to say, "It happened after this that the people of Moab with the people of Ammon, and others with them besides the Ammonites, came to battle against Jehoshaphat."

When the enemy comes to battle against us, it is critical that we are prepared. We must not let our guard down. The word *Moab* means *ease*. Many times the enemy will move back and let us think all is well, and then attempt to hit us with a knockout blow.

When I was a senior in high school, I was really a sports fanatic. I'm not sure how it happened, but I got into boxing. I knew almost nothing about the sport when I climbed in the ring for my first match. I came to my corner after the first round, red-faced, dazed, wondering why that guy was hitting me so much. The coach looked at me and said, "You might try to block one or two of those punches!" It did not take me long to understand with my gloves at my waist that my face was an open target. You see, in the excitement of the boxing match, I forgot to put my hands up. The next time the coach gave me a lesson on blocking punches, I listened. All through the Bible, we see illustrations of men and women who let their guards down, and Satan is always there for the knockout punch. Even David, a man after God's own heart, let his guard down at times, and the enemy was always there to take advantage of the situation. It is critical in our walk with God, to remember to keep our guard up.

The word *Ammon* means *people*. If we are not careful, we can allow people to be very discouraging and distracting. It is a big mistake to take our eyes off the Lord and put them on people. Verse 2 said that some came to Jehoshaphat, saying, "A great multitude is coming against you." Verse 3 says, "And Jehoshaphat feared." It is not abnormal for a person to fear, when they see not one, not even two, but several nations coming against them.

But Jehoshaphat did not let his fear dominate him. The Word says, "He set himself to seek the Lord." That literally means he set his face upon the Lord. And the word *set* means *a fixed position*. That is so important. We should have that fixed position on God every day, especially when we are under an attack of the enemy.

Often when people are under attack, they stop praying; they stop coming to church; they stop speaking God's Word. Rather than speaking faith and shouting in triumph to God for their victory, they begin speaking doubt; they begin magnifying the problem. They look at the circumstance in fear, rather than moving in faith toward God. Jehoshaphat fixed his eyes on God. And remember, when you look at God, even several armies coming at you will look small.

Jehoshaphat then proclaimed a fast throughout all of Judah. We know the power of fasting. The Bible says, "more over, when you fast." I like to think of it this way, when you pray and fast, you are going to do *more*, and it's going to put you *over*. In verse 4, all of Judah gathered together to ask help from the Lord. Then Jehoshaphat led them in a prayer, a prayer of faith, standing on God's promises. Verses 5 through 12 record the entire prayer, but here is how he ended it, "For we have no power against this great multitude that is coming against us; nor do we know what to do, but our eyes are upon You."

It is easy to look down when we are going through a battle, but looking down brings depression. Our view becomes distorted and we try looking at God through the eyes of our situation. If we look out when we are under attack, all we see is the enemy and looking out brings discouragement. The word *discourage* means *to lose heart*. The truth of the matter is this: Looking down and looking out will never change our situation. We need to look up, realizing that God is above all. And the good news is, the enemy can never cut off our source.

When Fanny Jane Crosby was a small child, she had an irritation in her eyes. Her family brought her to a man who claimed to be a doctor, but in fact was a fake. He put hot mustard in her eyes, and it blinded her. Fanny grew up sightless, but during her lifetime she wrote many of the most anointed hymns ever penned. One of my favorites is "*Blessed Assurance, Jesus Is Mine.*" In an interview later in life a reporter said to her, "Your songs are all over the world, but what a pity that you are blind." Do you know what she said? "Don't pity me, for the first face I shall see is Jesus." The one line in "*Blessed Assurance*" takes on new meaning when you know her story. It goes like this, "*Visions of rapture now burst on my sight. Watching and waiting, looking above.*"

Fanny Jane Crosby was not looking down. She was looking up. Her eyes were on the Lord. Jehoshaphat and the people of Judah were not looking out. They were looking up. They said to God, "Our eyes are upon You." We need to do the same thing they did. We need to keep our eyes upon the Lord.

We received a letter from a lady in Pennsylvania. She wrote: "My husband was suffering terribly from a back injury that he initially received during a training mission when he was a Navy Seal. He underwent tests, including an MRI, which indicated that two discs in his back weren't simply bulging or slipped. They had ruptured. The stuff from his disc was acting like a destructive acid on his nerves. If something wasn't done soon, he faced permanent loss of the use of his legs. The only way to correct the problem was surgery. You came to our church and when you gave the altar call, my husband was assisted to the altar. You prayed for him and he was able to walk out of the church that night without assistance. Within a few weeks he felt completely better and wanted to return to work. But his doctors didn't want to release him to return to work. He postponed the surgery and was no longer taking any pain medication. His doctors thought this was due to his fear of surgery. So they ran another MRI, then another. Completely astounded by what they saw; the discs were no longer leaking. They were full and in proper alignment."

And I love this part, "The doctors didn't know what to make of it. The specialists were almost angry because they didn't understand what had happened. According to medical understanding and treatments, there is no way to save a disc that is ruptured as badly as his was. God healed his back."

I respect doctors, my wife and I have many friends who are physicians, but doctors can only give you the facts. God's Word is the truth, and the truth will change the facts.

Verse 13 says, "Now all Judah with their little ones, their wives, and their children, stood before the Lord." The word *stood* means to *stand with expectancy*. So what do you do right now when you are under attack? You get your eyes on God. You fast and pray. You pray in faith, standing on God's promises, expecting God to answer your prayer. Verse 14 says, "Then the Spirit of the Lord came."

My first trip to Jamaica, in 1981, was as a representative of Christ For The Nations. As a young evangelist, I was excited about the opportunity to preach in a foreign country. I was asked to speak at a healing service in Kingston, one of their major cities. At the end of the service, several hundred people came forward for prayer. I was the evangelist praying for them, and they were building my faith. They would walk up to me and say something like this, "Preacher, the Bible says by His stripes I am healed, and if you will lay your hands on me, God is going to heal me." And God healed those people!

Many of us need a spiritual *facelift*. Instead of looking down into depression or looking out at the enemy of circumstance, we need to look up and allow the redemption of God to come to us. We need to stand with expectancy. Remember God is always moved by faith.

Chapter 7

Shouting is Celebrating

The Bible says, when all Judah stood before the Lord, the Spirit of the Lord came. Then God spoke to them. Look what He said in verse 15. "Listen, all you of Judah." Remember, Judah means praise. He is basically saying, "Listen, all you of praise." He is not just talking *about* praise; He is talking *to* praise. "Listen all you of praise, and you inhabitants of Jerusalem, and you, King Jehoshaphat! Thus says the Lord to you. 'Do not be afraid nor dismayed because of this great multitude, for the battle is not yours, but God's.'" God was telling them not to be afraid. This battle was not even theirs to fight. In verse 17, He said, "You will not need to fight in this battle. Position yourselves, stand still and see the salvation of the Lord."

When I first read "stand still and see the salvation of the Lord," I did not get it. Then I saw in the sixth chapter of Ephesians that God said, "and having done all, to stand." And I was more confused. But I was looking at it through a boxer's mentality. I had 44 amateur fights and became a Golden Glove champion in Fort Worth, Texas. After working out for two years, several hours a day, the thrill of being a champion lasted about three or four days. It did not take long at all for the excitement to wear off. So after I won Golden Gloves, for approximately two months, I did not bother working out. Every day during that time period, people were patting me on the back saying to me, "Man, you're the champ. You're good." Did it go to my head? Yeah, I was feeling really good about myself.

Then I got the phone call to go to Oklahoma City to fight in a pro-am tournament. I had been chosen as one of the fighters to appear in one of the amateur fights. So I went up there. Remember, I had not worked out in two months. They got me gloved up, and led me out. About that time, on one side of my peripheral, I see a guy who looks like a giant coming out the other side of the door. I said, "Who's that guy?"

They said, "That's who you're going to fight."

I said, "What?"

At that time I was a welterweight. The other guy was a light heavyweight. The guy I was supposed to fight did not show, so they just threw the incredible hulk into the ring with me. I mean that he was huge! The champion from Texas who hadn't bothered to workout for two months was certainly not in shape to fight this guy. Let me tell you something about boxing. Boxing is not a team sport. I do not care how many times a coach tells you he is in there with you. He is lying through his teeth.

I got in that ring and after the first round, my get up and

go, got up and left. Second round, I'm still alive, but I don't know how. I wasn't even thinking about winning anymore, I was just thinking about surviving. I remember after the second round I went back to the corner and my coach broke some smelling salts and put it right up in my nose. Smelling salts is pure ammonia. If you sniff pure ammonia, it will make you jerk back, but I just stood there, dazed.

My coach was such a motivator. He said, "Man, he hasn't even laid a glove on you."

I said, "You'd better check the referee because somebody's beating my brains out in there."

The third round I started praying, "Please, Lord, don't let him knock me out."

After that fight, I got out of the business.

When I read in the scripture having done all to stand, stand, all I could see was me as that young boxer with wobbly legs, hanging onto the ropes.

Then God said, "That's not what I mean when I say to stand. I want you to stand still and see!" God wants us to stand still, not in defeat, but to stand still and watch as He goes into action. When God goes into action, He is undefeated. He always wins. He never loses. What was impossible is now possible. What was difficult is now easy.

"Then Jehoshaphat," in verse 18, "bowed his head with his face to the ground, and all of Judah and the inhabitants of Jerusalem bowed before the Lord, worshiping the Lord." Remember, the enemy still has them surrounded; they have not gone anywhere. The armies of several nations are encamped around them. And the Bible says in verse 19, "Then the Levites … stood up to praise the Lord God of

Israel with voices loud and high." What were they doing? They were shouting to God!

Remember what I said about Joshua and the children of Israel? God had them shout in the presence of their enemy. God will have you shout while you are facing the enemy. God will have you shout while you are under attack. Shouting is *celebrating our God and His victory!* What you are doing is done by faith. When you shout you are saying, "God, Your victory is absolute. It does not matter what the circumstances appear to be, my eyes are fixed on You as I watch and see You triumph over the enemy! When it's all said and done, when the dust is settled, You will be the winner. You will be the only one standing."

I do not remember much about boxing, but I do remember the winner is always the last guy standing. And that will always be God, the alpha and omega, the beginning and the end.

Now the story really gets illogical. The enemy is still surrounding them on every side, and in verse 21, Jehoshaphat "appointed those who should sing to the Lord, and who should praise the beauty of holiness, as they went out before the army and were saying: 'Praise the Lord, for His mercy endures forever.'" That is amazing. They are about to fight a battle, and Jehoshaphat is forming a choir! They are going to war, outnumbered, with the enemy surrounding them, and rather than working on a strategy, making sure their weapons are ready, pumping up their warriors, they are putting a choir together!

The key to understanding this story is remembering that Jehoshaphat is the king of Judah, and Judah means praise. The enemy knew if he could defeat Judah, he could silence praise to God, but God used praise to knock out the enemy.

Verse 22 continues the story, "Now when they began to sing and to praise." The literal translation is, "When they began to shout and sing a praise song, the Lord set ambushes against the people of Ammon, Moab and Mount Seir, who had come against Judah; and they were defeated."

When Judah shouted and began to sing a praise song, the Lord Himself set ambushes against the enemy. And when God goes into action, the battle is over.

God not only defeated the enemy, but according to verse 23, He put them in confusion. Therefore the enemy began fighting and destroying one another.

Do you understand what God is showing us? As we praise the Lord with a shout of victory, not only will He defeat our enemy, but He will also put them in confusion. They will be busy destroying one another as we go into the north, south, east and west with the good news of the gospel.

And I love verse 25, "When Jehoshaphat and his people came to take away their spoil, they found among them an abundance of valuables on the dead bodies, and precious jewelry, which they stripped off for themselves, more than they could carry away." Think about this. "They were three days gathering the spoil, (the valuables) because there was so much." Three armies came against them; it took one day per army to gather the treasure God took for them from the enemy.

In Joel 2:25, God told the people He would restore

back the years the locust had stolen. This promise still stands today. Your children, your loved ones, your health, your marriage, your finances can all be restored to you.

Jehoshaphat and the people returned to Jerusalem with joy, according to verse 27, "for the Lord had made them rejoice over their enemies." Verse 28, "So they came to Jerusalem with stringed instruments, and harps and trumpets, to the House of the Lord."

Even though it does not specifically talk about shouting on their way to Jerusalem, I'm sure they were celebrating. Celebration and victory are always accompanied by shouting.

Chapter 8

Shouting Brings Healing

A man who owned an insurance company came to me for prayer. He told me, "I'm faithful to God with my tithe and offerings, but my business is about to go under."

I told him, "Let's shout over it." So we began shouting. That was on Sunday. On Monday, the very next day, his phone rang off the wall with new business. This man shared an office with another insurance agent, and the other man's phone did not ring one time that day. What an opportunity to witness the faithfulness of God!

Psalm 100:1 says, "Make a joyful noise to the Lord." The word *noise* means *shout!* Make a joyful shout to the Lord. Begin to see His promise, His victory, and your breakthrough. Seek the Lord and stand with expectancy while you are waiting on Him.

I prayed for a young woman recently who had been suffering from migraines so badly that it was hard for her to get out of bed. I told her, "There are many times when

God has healed me from pain instantly. But there have also been other times when God gave me the revelation on the inside that I was healed, but the manifestation did not come immediately."

I continued, "That is when I would stand on the promise." Then I told her this story. "I remember a time in my life when the blood vessel in my right eye would break, causing my eyeball to be streaked with red. Almost every week, I would have this problem with my eye. One day I prayed, and I heard the Lord say in my spirit, "I have healed you." And yet, for the next two weeks, my eye continued to hurt and be red. But every time I looked in the mirror I would say, "Eye, you are healed in Jesus' name." After two weeks my eye cleared up, and I have not had even one broken blood vessel since then. It is all about expectancy and believing that what God says He will do, will always happen."

There is a very familiar scripture in Zechariah 4:6, "This is the word of the Lord to Zerubbabel." If you study types and meanings in the Old Testament, you will understand that Zerubbabel was a type of Christ. The word of the Lord came to the people through the prophet, "Not by might, nor by power, but by My Spirit, says the Lord." As we read on, we see in verse 7, "Who are you, O great mountain? Before Zerubbabel you shall become a plain! And he shall bring forth the capstone, with shouts of 'grace, grace to it.'" In other words, God said he would shout, and that mountain would be removed.

My niece, Kenda, and her husband have wanted a child for seven years. All attempts to become pregnant had failed. She had been prayed over countless times, but to no avail.

This couple was facing a mountain of disappointment; no baby and no future hope of ever having one.

I preached on *"SHOUT"* at the church they attend. At the end of the service she came forward. Interestingly, she came for prayer over a job opportunity. She is a certified teacher and she had not been able to find a job fitting her qualifications. I shouted over her for that job, but then looked at her and said, "Kenda, listen to your Uncle Billy, I also shouted over that baby." She agreed with me with as much enthusiasm as she could. She had been prayed for over and over. Her level of hope was very low.

Nine days later, she discovered she was pregnant! Then one day later, she was offered a teaching job at a good school. Madison Nicole, a beautiful baby girl, was just born to this lovely couple. Our family, especially my brother, is celebrating the goodness of God. That mountain of disappointment was finally removed.

I was in Benton, Kentucky, and a man said to me, "Before I became a Christian, I accumulated a lot of debt as I was a bad steward with my money. My past credit history is poor. I've been a Christian for several years now and I am faithful with my tithe and offerings." He continued, "My wife and I have never owned a home and we are in the process of purchasing one. Last Friday, the mortgage company told us our credit rating was too low."

I said, "Let's shout over it." So we began shouting.

Monday, the very next day, the mortgage company telephoned. "We do not understand this, but your credit rating has gone up. Come sign the papers. The house is yours!"

A true worshiper worships God before He comes, not just when He comes. Don't just shout when you need God's help. Psalm 40:16 says, "May those who love Your salvation repeatedly shout, 'The Lord is great!'" Say it every day because you love His salvation.

When I was in Canada, the Lord said, "I want you to shout over the enemy." He said, "Shout over your situation, shout over your family, your health, your finances, your job, your church." Why? Because when we shout to God, we are shouting over the mountains we face. Because God is over all, He is far above everything.

In Mesquite, Texas, a lady came forward for prayer. This is what she said. "The owner of the house I'm renting told me he will evict me tomorrow." She continued, "I have looked for a job for months now, and I just cannot find one. I had a great job before and lost it. I have no money, and am about to lose my home. I do not know what to do."

I said, "Let's shout to God. Let's not look at the problem; let's look to the answer. Let's proclaim God's victory over this situation."

She did. Monday morning she received a call from the owner who knew nothing about the shouting. He said, "I was obviously in a bad mood Friday to threaten eviction. I would never force you to leave your home. I realize you are looking for a job. Please do not worry, I will work with you." That was Monday. Tuesday, she was offered a great job.

That night in Canada, the service was closing when the pastor asked me if I had anything else to say. It was at that moment I heard God say, "Shout to it, shout over your son."

I came to the front, told them what God had said, and went to the back of the church. As I was leaving the building, a man stopped me. Here is what he told me. "It is interesting you would use the words 'shout to it'. A couple of weeks ago I was in a maximum-security prison where, because of God's favor, I am allowed to preach the gospel. We had approximately 150 inmates in this particular service when suddenly, spontaneously, they began to shout. While the men were shouting, the back door flew open. I was the only one who could see what was happening, as I was standing on a stage in the front of the room.

I watched as six guards came into the room with one prisoner, chains from the top to bottom on him. This man had attacked one of the guards, and the warden did not know what to do with him. So he told the guards to chain him, and bring him to the service. He said maybe the preacher could help him. So they set him in the back row, with guards on each side.

Suddenly, these men, without knowing this prisoner had even been brought in, began to shout with even more passion. It became a great shout to the Lord. The shouting continued for approximately thirty minutes. By the time the service was over, the man who had been in chains was completely set free by the Lord."

Psalm 47:1 tells us, "Clap your hands, all you peoples! Shout to God with a voice of triumph." If we are not careful, we only obey the first part of that scripture, which is to clap our hands. But it goes on to say that we should shout to God. Shouting is not just about making noise. It is about *lifting our voice in triumph*. The next time you praise God by clapping your hands, remember to shout to Him with a voice of triumph.

SECTION THREE

Shout Into His Presence

At His sanctuary I will offer sacrifices with shouts of joy, singing and praising the Lord with music.
Psalm 27:6

Chapter 9

Shouting is Praise

David is the only person in the Bible who was described as "a man after God's own heart." In many ways his life was a revelation of what we could expect from the Messiah. He was a type or shadow of Christ. David gave passionate praise to God. One of his key characteristics was the purity of his worship. He was not ashamed to allow others to observe him as he joyfully, opened his life in adoration to the Lord. Would this not be a wonderful attribute with which to model your life of praise and worship? Rather than allowing a person, or even an organization, to place limitations on your patterns of praise, why not study men like David, of whom it was said by God, "He is a man after My own heart, a man who will do My will."

I never realized until I began purposefully, studying on shouting, how often it is mentioned in the Bible, and to what extent it will be heard in Heaven. In 2 Samuel 6, a story is told concerning David as he returned the Ark of the Covenant to Jerusalem. David, the man who had killed the enemy Goliath while still a young man, was now king of Israel. God had anointed David, through Samuel, to become king while he was still a young shepherd boy. But years passed; many difficult years, before the total manifestation occurred in his life.

Before becoming king of all Israel, David first, was crowned to rule only a portion of the kingdom, that being Judah. He ruled Judah for seven years. I love the beauty of God's Word, as there are multifaceted truths hidden between the lines. David was king of Judah for seven years. *Seven* is the number that represents *perfection*. The word *Judah* means *praise*. God's grace was upon David. When He looked at him, He saw *perfect praise*. After David's life demonstrated perfect praise, he was immediately elevated to king over all Israel.

High on David's agenda, when he was crowned king of Israel, was bringing the Ark of the Covenant to Jerusalem. The Ark of the Covenant was a literal representation of the presence of the Lord. David realized it had been neglected during the reign of King Saul, the last king. In 1 Chronicles 13:3, David said, "Let us bring the ark of our God back to us for we have not inquired of it since the days of Saul." This scripture is a reminder to us that Saul knew and understood God's power, but he never pursued God's presence. David wanted the presence of God in his life. Many chase after the power of God without ever attempting to live in His presence, but God's presence brings His power.

2 Samuel 6:15 says, "David and all the house of Israel

brought up the ark of the Lord with shouting and with the sound of the trumpet." Isn't that amazing? God could have chosen many ways for man to usher in His presence, but He chose shouting.

Psalm 100:2 says, "Come before His presence with singing." The word *singing* used in this scripture means *a ringing cry* or *a shout*. Do you understand God's purpose in having us come before His presence with shouting? It is because He lives in victory. We are to celebrate our God and His victory. You may look at the circumstance of your life at this moment and ask, "How can I shout to God when everything is going wrong for me?" You can shout because He has the power, ability and willingness to make those things right in your life.

David brought up the ark of God with shouting. Some may think it is foolish to shout, but God loves exuberant praise. In 1 Corinthians 1:25, the writer tells us, "The foolishness of God is wiser than men." Even in our praise we need to move in the wisdom of God, as there is a vast difference between the foolishness of God and the foolishness of man.

Let me explain. I was in Wal-Mart one day when a man came in wearing a headset, singing as loudly as he could. He looked like he was crazy and he really could not sing at all. Unfortunately, he was singing a Christian song. When I looked at him, I thought he thought he was witnessing for God. But he was not. People were running to avoid him. The foolishness of God is wiser than man. The foolishness of God brings God results ... while the foolishness of man is just foolish! If God is in it, it may look foolish to the world, but it is not foolish at all.

My brother, Bruce, who is a worship leader in a church in Mesquite, Texas, was praying with me for a young lady who attended his church. This woman was in her early twenties, and was incredibly bright. She had been offered scholarships to leading universities across the country, but could not accept them because of severe depression. Her marriage was in jeopardy, and she had been contemplating suicide. I laid my hands on her and began praying when suddenly, she released a shout and a scream to God. When she did that, Bruce and I both jumped back because it caught us off guard. Everyone in the church heard her, and I am sure many thought she was out of order. She wrote my brother a few weeks later and said, "God healed me of depression. He has given me back my life. I have no more suicidal tendencies, my marriage is healed, and I have accepted a full scholarship at a major university."

The foolishness of God is wiser than man.

I was ministering in Burleson, Texas, on the subject of dancing before the Lord. A lady who had been suffering from MS for years was seated in the back of the church. Her doctor had told her there was no cure for the disease. Her body was deteriorating. She had no reflexes. She could not even touch her nose with her finger. Almost every movement that we take for granted, this lady could not perform. The entire time I was ministering on dancing before the Lord, she was questioning this word until the close of the service when she heard the Lord speak, "Will you dance for Me?"

She said, "Yes, Lord, I will dance for You." She grasped

the pew in front, pulled her body up, and began to move her toes up and down, as that was all the strength she had. She went home that night, all the symptoms of MS still intact. But when she woke the next morning, every indication of the disease was gone. And they have been gone for eight years.

I returned recently to that church. This lady came to tell me her story. She said, "I have full strength. None of the symptoms of MS has ever returned. My doctor would not release me for several months because he could not believe what had happened. He finally agreed, saying, 'I cannot explain this. There is no cure for MS. This is a miracle.' There was even an article in the newspaper of my healing."

Shouting, while ushering in His presence, is very appropriate. Obviously, God likes it. He likes celebrating. I wonder why it feels so strange, and even uncomfortable in our society. Have you noticed it is not uncomfortable to shout at ball games? We don't walk away from events like that thinking how crazy the people acted over their favorite teams. I never left one of Lance's or Jared's ball games feeling embarrassed or self-conscious because I shouted. My friends, sitting around me, never acted uncomfortable at my expressive nature. They cheered with me. The more excited I got, the more excited they got.

Lucifer led worship in heaven before his fall. He saw the value of worship better than any other created being. That is why he wants it for himself. The greatest counterfeit tool of Satan today is worship. What is normal in the world, shouting and celebrating, becomes abnormal in the church. Do you see how we have allowed the enemy to twist things? We celebrate in the world, but stand quietly before God. The Lord wants our praise. He wants our celebration. It is time to restore back the worship that pleases God.

Chapter 10

Shouting in Faith

Every morning, when I begin to pray, the first thing I do is shout to the Lord. Obviously, there are times when I am traveling and staying in hotels, that it would not be appropriate to shout out loud. At that time, God gets my inner shout. But it is always passionate. You see, God looks on the heart. He knows our intentions. Saying this, I also know we sometimes use this as an excuse. "I will praise Him in my heart," we might say, "but I am not going to show any outward expression."

The word *praise* means *an expression*. There are certain things you cannot do in your heart. You cannot clap your hands in your heart. Think about this, if I did everything just within my heart, I could play the piano! I could play the drums! I could lead worship! In my heart! Therefore, even though there are times when common sense cautions me not to be loud, it does not stop me from shouting. I certainly never want to allow my witness and testimony to upset others, but when I praise the Lord, and the circumstances do not prevent it, I shout to Him with a loud voice. When we shout to the Lord we do not have to be obnoxious or try to destroy our voices. We should just *lift our voices in triumphant praise.* And while one person could be loud and boisterous, another person might use a more gentle tone, depending on their personality. The key is to praise Him. Shouting will usher you into His presence.

Solomon, David's son, obviously watched his father and learned by example. When he built that magnificent temple to God, look at what the scripture says about the dedication ceremony. 2 Chronicles 5:13-14, "Indeed it came to pass, when the trumpeters and singers were as one, to make one sound to be heard in praising and thanking the Lord, and when they lifted up their voice," remember, lifting your voice means to shout, "and when they lifted their voice with the trumpets and cymbals and instruments of music, and praised the Lord, saying." Here is what they were shouting out, " 'For He is good, for His mercy endures forever,' that the house, the house of the Lord, was filled with a cloud, so that the priests could not continue ministering because of the cloud; for the glory of the Lord filled the house of God."

Can you imagine shouting as one voice before the Lord in such a way that the glory of the Lord filled His house? I was in a service one night when the glory of the Lord suddenly settled over the crowd. No one moved. Children, who would have usually been wiggling, sat still in the presence of God. The glory was there about forty-five minutes, and when it lifted, salvation had come to the house. Many had been saved, healed, and set free.

When God's presence is felt, no one wants to leave. I was in a church in Farmington, New Mexico. The service began at six o'clock, and at ten, the power of God had fallen on the place. People everywhere were praying and crying out to God. I saw the youth pastor weeping with tears flowing down his face. I put my hand on his back and prayed for him, not even knowing what he was praying about. I moved to the other side of the building where the pastor was standing. Remember, it was after ten o'clock, and the people were not going home. We laughed as one of us said, "Isn't God good? Look what He has done tonight."

I told him, "Your youth pastor is over there just weeping. God has really touched him."

"He cannot be crying." The pastor informed me, "When he was just a child, the doctors discovered a tumor on his brain. And although the operation was successful, his tear ducts dried up. He cannot cry. He spends anywhere from $60 to $70 a month for special eye drops, just to lubricate his eyes."

This young man, twenty-three years old, a second-generation minister, loved God with all his heart, but there were days he could not get out of bed, even with eye drops, because his eyes would be so irritated. I told the pastor, "Well, they sure looked like tears to me." About that time, the youth pastor turned and looked at his wife, then at us, tears flowing down his face.

His wife began shouting. He began shouting. The pastor began shouting. Then the young man danced around the church. At midnight the pastor told him,

"We've got to lock the church, it is time to go."

The young man said, "Lock me in. I'm not going anywhere!" God completely healed him while he was shouting in His presence.

Matthew 21:12-14, "Then Jesus went into the temple of God and drove out all those who bought and sold in the temple, and overturned the tables of the money changers and the seats of those who sold doves. And He said to them, 'It is written, My house shall be called a house of prayer, but you have made it a den of thieves.' Then the blind and the lame came to Him in the temple, and He healed them. But when the chief priests and scribes saw the wonderful things that He did, and the children crying out in the temple and saying, 'Hosanna to the Son of David!' they were indignant and said to Him, 'Do you hear what these are saying?' And Jesus said to them, 'Yes. Have you never read, Out of the mouth of babes and nursing infants You have perfected praise?'" Do you know what the Lord was saying? These children are shouting out praise to Me, and they have perfect praise!

Children are so beautiful, and yet very humorous at times too. I was preaching in Mesquite, Texas, just east of Dallas, and a friend of ours brought her seven-year-old daughter, Lauren, to the service. They sat on the front row and the little girl listened intently to this message on *"SHOUT."*

The following week our friend was shopping with her daughter for school clothes at the mall. Passing a shop that pierced ears, Lauren tugged on her Mom's arm, wanting to get her ears pierced.

"No, some other time," her mother told her. "We are here for school clothes."

"Well, I'm just going to shout to the Lord then!" Lauren told her.

"What in the world are you talking about?" Her mother asked.

"Didn't you hear Billy Gibson? If you want something from God, just shout to Him."

I do not remember saying it exactly that way, but a month later, while telling me this story, my friend showed me a picture of Lauren. As I looked at the picture, I noticed her ears were pierced. You will never convince Lauren that shouting to the Lord does not work.

In Pennsylvania, I asked people to come forward that would like to be baptized in the Holy Spirit and receive their prayer language. The pastor's granddaughter came forward. That night the power of God fell on those who came for prayer, and it embraced her. She began to cry out to God. She began to shout to God. For several hours this young girl was caught up in the heavenlies. Even after the service, the peace of God just enveloped her. The following day one of her teachers telephoned her mom, "What is going on with your daughter? She is just a little bit too happy!"

Shouting into the presence of the Lord will definitely leave us happy. We come into His presence with shouting. We usher in His presence with shouting. We dedicate His church with shouting. And we, as His children, can release perfect praise. So let us become one sound and one praise and one shout to God in unity and see what the Lord will do.

We have friends who pastor in California. On Saturday evening, before we were to minister in their church, they took Marsha and me out to eat. When we asked them about their children, they told us their daughter had left home when she graduated from high school and had moved in with a young man. She was not living for God and their hearts were broken.

Her father told us, "There have been many times I've contemplated quitting the ministry because I feel like such a failure as a father."

Marsha and I knew that our time with them was a divine appointment. On Sunday morning, I shared the testimony of my son Jared. As we ministered during the week, you could hear this couple shouting to the Lord over their daughter.

Two weeks later we received a telephone call from the mother. "Our daughter called this morning and said, 'Mama, I don't want to live this way anymore. Can I move home for a little while until I can get my life straight? I want to get right with God.'"

She came home with a repentant heart. I talked to her father recently. He told me that she is now working in their children's church. God is so good!

Psalm 29:9 says, "In His temple everyone shouts, 'Glory!'" And again in Psalm 27:6, David says, "At His tabernacle I will offer sacrifices with shouts of joy, singing and praising the Lord with music."

Many times our attitude is Lord, You bring the miracle, then I will shout. Lord, You bring the healing, then I will shout. Lord, You bring the answer to prayer, then I will shout. Lord, You save this lost loved one, and then I will shout. But in return God is saying, "Go ahead and shout now!" When we shout, we release faith and it takes faith to shout when you see the enemy surrounding you. It takes faith to shout and keep your eyes on God when it looks as though everything is impossible and will never change. It takes faith to shout when the doctor's report says an incurable disease. When we shout we are saying, "Lord, I am celebrating Your victory in this healing. I am celebrating Your victory in this lost loved one's life. I am celebrating Your victory in my finances." Whatever your challenge is, celebrate God's victory in it. And when you do, God will not let you down. He always comes through. God never fails.

In Raleigh, North Carolina, I prayed with a woman who brought her young daughter forward. She told me, "My daughter was diagnosed on Friday with sleep apnea. This disease causes you to stop breathing while asleep."

I told her, "Let's just shout to God over your daughter." And we did.

That Sunday evening she put the child to bed early, so she would be rested for school the next day. She and her husband were watching television when she suddenly sat up straight in her chair and told him, "Hit the mute, hit the mute!"

She had frightened him, "What is the matter with you? Do you hear someone trying to break in?"

She said, "No, listen. Turn the sound off." He muted the television.

"I don't hear anything," he told her.

"Don't you get it? There is no noise."

This lady told me later, "As long as my daughter has been alive she has snored so loudly you could hear her all through the house." She was not snoring that night. For the first time in nine years, they heard silence. God is a miracle worker!

Shouting is not just making noise. It is celebrating. Look at any fan when their team is winning. You can see it on their face. You can tell it by their expression. They are celebrating! They are not mad. They are glad. That is an attitude that you and I must develop when it comes to God. "Lord, I celebrate Your victory. I celebrate Your greatness."

Every morning when you pray, begin with celebrating. Celebrate His victory, celebrate His presence. See what God will do. He will make a way where there is no way. He will make the impossible possible. We prayed with a woman in Arkansas who had been told by her doctor she had a cancerous mass in her breast. After shouting to the Lord, she went back to the doctor. She was rechecked eight times. No mass. The doctor said to her, "I cannot explain this, I do not understand. It is not there."

When you shout, shout out victories! Shout your boast in the Lord. Brag on Him. My deliverer. My banner. Great is the Lord. There is none like You. You may say, "Well, I don't always feel like shouting."

Do not base your shout on feelings. You do not live your life on feelings. You do not always feel like going to work, but you go. You do it as an act of your will. Any psychologist in the country will tell you this truth: Feelings follow action. If you will act right, the feelings will eventually catch up. I do not feel my way into acting right. I act my way into feeling right.

Many times, when I get up in the morning, I do not feel like shouting. But I do it anyway. That is why David talked to himself. He said, "Bless the Lord, oh my soul and all that is within me." I will bless the Lord. I will shout to the Lord. I will celebrate the victory of the Lord. In my bed at night, when I awake in the morning, in my automobile, on my job, in my leisure time, I will bless the Lord!

SECTION FOUR

A Progressive Shout

*Enter His gates with thanksgiving;
go into His courts with praise.
Give thanks to Him and praise His name.
Psalm 100:4*

Chapter 11

Shouting is Crying Out

As I have said before, in certain translations of the Bible, the word meaning *shout* may have been translated differently for easier comprehension and flow of scripture. To understand the progression of shout, the first meaning of shout, we want to look at is *to cry out* or *to cry out in distress*. Romans 8:14-15 says, "For as many as are led by the Spirit of God, these are the sons of God. For you did not receive the spirit of bondage again to fear, but you received the Spirit of adoption by whom we cry out, 'Abba, Father.'" *Abba* essentially means *father*, but expresses a much deeper affection and childlike trust in a parent, such as a papa or daddy. So when the writer of Romans tells us we can shout out *Abba, Father*, he is telling us *to cry out to our Papa*.

I have two granddaughters. Taylor is six and Bailee is three. They bring a lot of joy to my life. I told my son, not too long ago, if I had known grand babies were going to be this much fun, I would have had them first!

Recently, I was visiting with my son Lance in his home. The girls were upstairs playing when I heard Bailee cry out. I jumped up and hurried toward the stairs. Lance did not even move. "Dad, it's nothing, she's just mad about something."

"Man, how can you tell?"

He said, "Oh, I just can."

A little later, we heard Bailee cry out again. "Now, that is something," he told me. We ran upstairs, found she had fallen and hurt herself, so we prayed for her.

As parents, we learn to distinguish the cry of our children, whether they are crying because they are hurting or they are just being temperamental. Our Heavenly Father also knows by our cry when we sincerely need His help and when we are just whining or complaining.

My mother absolutely would not tolerate whining or complaining. Can you imagine a house full of nine kids, all whining at the same time? But let one of us cry out in pain, and she was there. She knew by the tone of our voice when we needed her.

Our Heavenly Father is no different. When you cry out to Him, He will be there for you. Psalm 34:16 says, "His ears are open to our cries."

"God is our refuge and strength, a very present help in trouble," according to Psalm 46:1. I like that. No matter the time or the place, God is available to help us when we cry out to Him.

Recently I was scheduled to minister in a church in Tulsa, Oklahoma. On Friday afternoon, before I left town,

I called the church office and spoke with the Pastor's secretary. She told me, "Brother Gibson, Pastor has just been rushed to the emergency room. We do not know what is wrong with him, but he is in a lot of pain." Later that evening, I received a phone call telling me that the pastor was still in tremendous pain and an ultrasound had revealed a kidney stone that he needed to pass.

On Saturday, after I arrived in Tulsa, I received a call from the pastor. "Billy, I'm not sure I can be in the service tomorrow." His pain was so intense I could hardly understand his words.

"That's okay," I reassured him, "We will have a good service, and will pray for you."

But on Sunday morning he came to church. It was apparent that he was still in tremendous pain. Obviously, he had not passed the kidney stone.

Sunday morning my message was on *"SHOUT."* In the evening service, the pastor was standing by the altar, when suddenly he began to jump up and down, shouting to the Lord.

After service I asked him, "What happened? You look like a totally different person from the one who came into the building this morning."

He told me, "All the pain is gone."

It stayed gone. Monday; Tuesday; Wednesday. On Wednesday afternoon, he had an appointment for another ultrasound. The doctor could not find the kidney stone. It was gone, but it never passed from his body. He cried to God and God heard his cry.

Jesus teaches us through a parable in Luke 18:1 that

men ought to always pray and not lose heart, give up or quit. He tells this story. "There was in a certain city a judge who did not fear God nor regard man. Now there was a widow in the city, and she came to him, saying, 'Get justice for me from my adversary.' And he would not for a while, but afterward he said within himself, 'Though I do not fear God nor regard man, yet because this widow troubles me I will avenge her, lest by her continual coming she weary me.'" Look at what happened. In the beginning the judge ignored the widow's request, but she just kept coming. The story doesn't say how many times she came knocking on the man's door. She could have come for weeks, or even years. The judge, who did not fear God or man, eventually did what the widow asked because her continual coming wore him out.

This story illustrates the value of persistent prayer. In verse 6, Jesus said, "Hear what the unjust judge said. And shall not God avenge His own elect who cry out day and night to Him, though He bears long with them? I tell you that He will avenge them speedily." Many of us miss the point of this teaching when we pray. If we do not immediately receive what we asked for in prayer, we are disappointed. Yet Jesus said we are to cry out day and night. If we do this, our Father will avenge us.

People often ask me, "How long do I knock on the door?" I tell them, "Until He opens it."

The scripture found in Matthew 7:7 literally means *ask and keep on asking; seek and keep on seeking; knock and keep on knocking.* When you ask, you will receive; when you seek, you will find; when you knock, the door will open.

The key is to keep on keeping on until God answers.

Bruce Wilkinson, the author of *"The Prayer of Jabez,"* explains the urgency of Jabez' plea for the Lord to bless him indeed. The word *indeed* added to the prayer recorded in 1 Chronicles 4:10 means *intensely*. So when we read that Jabez called out to the Lord for His blessing, we know that he was crying out intensely.

Understanding what it is *to cry out to God in distress* is vital to recognizing the value of shouting unto God with a voice of triumph.

The second meaning of shout is *to lift your voice*. Whenever you see these words in the Bible, they mean to shout. We lift our voice in thanksgiving and praise.

A word used more than any of the other seven Hebrew words to define praise is *halal*. Halal means *to shine, to boast, to celebrate*. The word hallelujah is a derivative of the word halal. *Hallelujah* stands for halal to Yahweh, which means *to praise or to celebrate God*.

Ezra 3:11 says, "All the people shouted with a great shout, when they praised the Lord." The word *praised* in this verse is defined as *halal*.

Zephaniah 3:14 says, "Sing, O daughter of Zion!" The word translated *sing* in Hebrew means *to shout aloud* or *shout for joy*. And then it goes on to say, "Shout, O Israel! Be glad and rejoice with all your heart, O daughter of Jerusalem! The Lord has taken away your judgments, He has cast out your enemy. The king of Israel, the Lord, is in your midst; You shall see disaster no more. In that day it shall be said to Jerusalem: 'Do not fear; Zion, let not your hands be weak. The Lord your God in your midst,

The Mighty One, will save; He will rejoice over you with gladness, He will quiet you with His love, He will rejoice over you with singing.'" What is the prophet saying? Why should we shout? Why should we celebrate? We celebrate because God is in our midst. When we cry out to Papa, He hears our cry.

I was in Oklahoma City preaching on *"SHOUT"* one Sunday morning when a man came down for prayer who was suffering from depression and schizophrenia. We prayed over him, shouting victory for his life. In the Sunday evening service, I heard someone behind me rejoicing in a shout before God. I could not see who it was, but the person sounded victorious. When the service ended I was informed it was this same man. He told me, "God has broken depression off my life. The schizophrenia is gone."

When I was a teenager, I would often come home late at night. As I passed my mother's bedroom, I could hear her praying, shouting, and crying out to God for her kids. "Lord," she would say, "You promised me all of my children would be saved. I believe You, Lord."

Before I got right with God, I used to tell my mother, "Mama, you're messing up my life. You're messing up my parties." And she would just smile. I figured out later telling her that was like throwing gasoline on a fire. She would just go off and pray more. She knew the value of crying out to the Lord.

I tell people, "If you have a mother or grandmother praying for you, you had better just give it up!"

Chapter 12

Shouting Defeats the Giant

A third meaning of shout is *to give a war cry over the enemy*. In 1 Samuel 4, Israel was in a battle with their enemy. Their adversary was winning, so the elders decided to bring the Ark of the Covenant to the battlefront. Verse 5 says, "And when the Ark of the Covenant of the Lord came into the camp, all Israel shouted so loudly that the earth shook." Can you imagine shouting so loudly that the earth would shake? Verse 6, "Now when the Philistines," they were the enemy, "heard the noise of the shout, they said, 'What does the sound of this great shout in the camp of the Hebrews mean?' Then they understood that the ark of the Lord had come into the camp." Verse 7, "So the Philistines were afraid."

This is a critical truth you must understand: When you release a war cry with a shout, it brings fear to the enemy.

When I was about twelve years old, my older brother Bobby talked my mother into letting me go with him to work during the summer. Bobby was the director of a park and recreation center. Summer then and summer now, for a twelve-year-old, is really different. Back in those days my mother would feed us breakfast and then say, "Get outside!" We either went to the front yard or the back yard to play and we stayed out all day. So when my brother gave me the opportunity to go with him to a park and recreation center, I jumped on it. I was excited.

He told me, "All I need you to do is help me out around here."

One day after a game of softball, Bobby told me, "I've got to go back in and do some things. If you would, stay out here and gather all the bases, bats and balls, and put them in the bag."

"No problem." Bobby left and I began to gather up the equipment. Suddenly, out of nowhere, three teenage boys appeared, standing directly in front of me. To a twelve-year-old, they looked like giants.

"Hey, kid, leave that stuff here." I froze like a deer in headlights.

They went on to say, "If you don't leave it here, we're going to take care of you."

I had a problem. I knew my brother told me to bring the equipment in, but I did not want to get killed. I just stood there. They started toward me, and I am thinking, "This is it, it's over." They took two or three steps, laughing, when all of a sudden they stopped dead in their tracks with a look of fear on their faces.

I was thinking, "What in the world happened?" Then I turned around and the answer was standing really, really tall, right behind me. BOBBY! Those guys took off running.

I yelled at them, "Come on back here, boys, let's do this!" I picked that bag up and stuck my chest out. Actually, I don't think I had a chest then, but I stuck it out anyhow. I walked back inside the recreation center like John Wayne with my big brother by my side.

Do you understand why I am telling you this story? There are times the enemy will endeavor to make you fearful. He was always attempting this with Israel: Look at the height of the walls around Jericho, rather than the power of God to knock them down. Look at the size of Goliath, rather than the size of God. Satan knows if he can get you to look at a problem, and see it is greater than you can handle, he has you.

Remember this story the next time the enemy magnifies the problem or tries to scare you. Take a deep breath and see who is standing right beside you. It is JESUS!

Then you can say, "Bring it on, boys!" Because when God arrives, His enemy scatters! Every time.

In Amos 1:14, the prophetic word of the Lord tells us there will be shouting in the day of battle. When the men of Judah gave a shout in 2 Chronicles 13:15, they released a war cry. In Joshua 6:20, when the people shouted with a great shout, it was a war cry they were releasing. When my son, Jared, was away from God, I looked at the circumstances and almost developed a mind set that things would never change. But after getting the word from God to shout over him, I did exactly that! Many times, driving down the road, I would begin to shout with a war cry! And that war cry brought fear to the enemy, because he knew God was going to bring the victory.

A fourth meaning of shout, we want to look at is *to shout for joy*. Think about it. We can shout *for joy*. If you need joy in your life, shout for it! Psalm 35:27 says, "Let them shout for joy and be glad." Psalm 100:1 tells us to "Make a joyful shout unto the Lord." I want to show you something that is simple, but profound. We learned earlier that shouting is praise to God. So as you shout for joy, which is praise, God uses our praise to develop joy in our lives. Psalm 100:4 says, "Enter into His gates with thanksgiving, and into His courts with praise." As you shout for joy, the shout takes you into God's presence because it is a shout of praise. And David said in Psalm 16:11, "In Your presence is fullness of joy."

I shout for joy; enter His presence; and receive the fullness of joy I need in my life!

Why do I need fullness of joy? Nehemiah 8:10 tells us, "The joy of the Lord is your strength." Again, I praise God; I shout for joy; go into His presence where there is fullness of joy. And that fullness of joy becomes the strength I need in life.

After ministering on *"SHOUT"* in a church in Oklahoma, on a Friday night, a woman in a wheelchair came forward to the altar for prayer. She had been in a wheelchair most of her life. As I approached her in the prayer line, I could hear her shouting to the Lord. She was shouting for victory and she was shouting for joy. She was very sincere in her praise to God. On Sunday morning the woman walked into church without her wheelchair. Healed. And she was still shouting for joy.

Psalm 132:16 says, "Shout aloud for joy!" A lady in Kentucky came forward for prayer. "I need a job. I've been looking for six months. I just graduated with a degree in sociology and I want to work in that field, but I cannot find anything."

I said, "Let's shout." We shouted.

She came back to church on Monday night and told me, "I received a job today where I can use my degree."

I have friends who pastor in Hawaii. Their former son-in-law was an agnostic. Even though the marriage had broken up, this couple still loved the young man and wanted to see him saved. During their entire relationship, he would never discuss religion with them. If they attempted to bring it up, he would quickly change the subject.

They began to shout over this young man. Day and night they cried out to God on his behalf. Two weeks later, the pastor's wife came to the mainland and was visiting in Texas where this young man lived. He heard she was close by, and telephoned her.

"Would you come for a visit? I want to talk to you."

When she arrived, he asked her, "Would you tell me how I can be saved?" This man was an agnostic, who would not discuss anything concerning God for more than ten years. Now he says, "Tell me how I can be saved."

She shared with him the scriptures on salvation.

"We were sitting at a kitchen table when I began to lead him in the sinner's prayer," she said, "He pushed his chair back and fell flat on his face and began weeping." God saved, delivered, and baptized him in the Holy Spirit. He is now a regular member of a church.

Psalm 5:11 says, "Let them ever shout for joy because You defend them."

Here is the progression: You cry to Papa, and Papa hears your cry. Then He comes on the scene. That is when you begin to lift up your voice with thanksgiving, praise and worship, because Papa is there. And when Papa is here, everything is going to be all right.

Do you know why the Levites could shout when they were surrounded and outnumbered by several nations? They were able to shout because Papa showed up in the camp. The Bible says He is for me, so who can be against me? Greater is He that is within me than He that is in the world. So I cry out to Papa and He comes on the scene. I lift up my voice with thanksgiving, praise and worship. And because He is on the scene, because I know He is there, I can release a war cry in faith against the enemy. Then God puts the enemy to flight and defeats him. Now that the enemy is defeated, I can walk away and shout for joy.

I want to give you an overview of the progression of the shout in 2 Chronicles 20. Verses 4 through 12, they cried out to Papa; verse 14, then the Spirit of the Lord came on the scene. Verse 19, the Levites lifted up their voices loud and high in thanksgiving, praise and worship to God. Then verse 22 tells us when they began to sing and shout and release a war cry, God defeated the enemy. Verse 27 says they returned to Jerusalem with joy.

The Word does not specifically say they shouted on their return trip to Jerusalem, but in my heart I believe they did. The Bible says they rejoiced over their enemies. And when people celebrate victory, they shout!

A pastor, who is a close friend of mine, has one child, a daughter. I, along with several other ministers, received a phone call to come and pray for her as she was in critical need. He told me, "Billy, my daughter has been sick for several months, and for the last week we've had her in the hospital." This young woman at that time had a six-week-old baby she could not even take care of. Her husband and parents were caring for the baby during her illness.

"The four specialists, assigned to her case, cannot agree on a diagnosis. One says she has spinal meningitis. Another one says she might have mono." He continued, "She has migraines so painful the doctors are giving her morphine. Just lifting her head off the bed causes her to throw up."

He shared that they were desperate, not knowing what to do for their only daughter. At five o'clock that afternoon, several ministers met at the hospital to pray.

Entering the room, we could see a look of death on this girl. We joined her family and began to cry out to Papa. Just recently, God had begun to give me this word on shouting. My son had just been set free. I shared it with the other ministers.

I told them, "I know we can't shout here in the hospital room. But as soon as we get into our automobiles, I want each of us to release a shout of celebration over this girl's healing."

Everyone agreed to do it. As soon as I entered my vehicle, I began to shout. Others telephoned me they were shouting. Then the Lord said to me, "In twenty-four hours I am going to turn her around." Twenty-four hours later this young mother walked out of the hospital healed.

Consider this: If you as a parent would be there at the cry of your children, how much more does our Father hear the cries of His children. If there are mountains of circumstances in your path to victory, do not despair. Begin to:

- Cry out to God expecting Him to hear you
- Lift your voice in thanksgiving and praise
- Release a war cry over the enemy
- Shout for joy as you celebrate God's victory.

SECTION FIVE

WHAT TO DO AFTER THE VICTORY

*He shouts with joy because
You give him victory.
Psalm 21:1*

Chapter 13

Shouting is Everlasting

You have shouted to the Lord. The victory has come. Now what? 2 Chronicles 20:26-30 says, "And on the fourth day they assembled in the Valley of Berachah, for there they blessed the Lord; therefore the name of that place was called The Valley of Berachah until this day. Then they returned, every man of Judah and Jerusalem, with Jehoshaphat in front of them, to go back to Jerusalem with joy, for the Lord had made them rejoice over their enemies. So they came to Jerusalem, with stringed instruments and harps and trumpets, to the House of the Lord. And the fear of God was on all the kingdoms of those countries when they heard that the Lord had fought against the enemies of Israel. Then the realm of Jehoshaphat was quiet, for his God gave him rest all around."

The enemy of Jehoshaphat had been soundly defeated by the Lord. There was victory in the camp. God's victory!

God had taken the praises of His people and turned

them into weapons that put the enemy to flight. No general, in any army today, would think to use the tactics God used that day. Psalm 2 tells us God sees when the kings and rulers of the earth take counsel together against Him. Verse 4 tells us what He does, "He who sits in the heavens shall laugh, the Lord shall hold them in derision." I get the feeling God laughed while watching the confusion of the enemy that day. And then I believe He observed carefully to see the reaction of those He had defended in battle. What did they do? What should they have done? What should you do when God wins a victory for you?

Number one. *You continue to bless the Lord.* When the Word says they assembled in the Valley of Berachah, it literally means they assembled in the *Valley of Blessing*. And there they blessed the Lord. Never forget what the Lord has done for you. Every time I look at my son, I remember what the Lord did in his life and thankfulness rises up inside me. I will continue to bless the Lord.

In Psalm 34:1, David said, "I will bless the Lord at all times; His praise shall continually be in my mouth." Deuteronomy 8:11 says, "Beware that you do not forget the Lord your God." How many people forget? There is a story in Luke 17 concerning ten lepers. They called to Jesus from afar off, and pled for mercy. Jesus, rich in compassion, healed them. One returned to thank Him. Jesus' question is still relevant today: "Were there not ten cleansed? But where are the nine?" After the victory, after the healing, after the answer to prayer, remember to bless the Lord.

Number two. *Be joyful in your restoration.* Verse 27 says, "Then they returned." Another meaning for the original word in the Hebrew for returned is *restored*. The people returned to their homes, restored. When I read that scripture, I heard the Lord speak to me, "Continue to shout over every one in your household. Not one of them will be lost." Acts 16:31 says, "Believe on the Lord Jesus Christ, and you will be saved, you and your household."

My mother prayed for all of her family. As a young man, I knew the majority of them were lost, but that did not prevent her from believing God's Word that her household would be saved. Many nights I came home late to the voice of my mama crying out to God for her family. At her funeral, every child had been won to Christ, with the exception of my oldest sister. Shirley gave her heart to God that day.

The Lord spoke to me as I watched my sister receive Jesus, "Son, your prayers will outlive you. So don't ever give up." Joel 2:25 says, "I will restore to you the years that the swarming locusts hath eaten." Restoration is a big part of the blessing of God.

"When Jehoshaphat and his people came to take away their spoil," in verse 25, "they found among them an abundance of valuables on the dead bodies, and precious jewelry, which they stripped off for themselves, more than they could carry away." Pay attention to this next verse. "They were three days gathering the spoil because there was so much."

Do you know what God said to me as I read this verse? He said, "As you begin to shout, I will restore back what the enemy has taken. You will see much come to you that has been stolen by the enemy." It took the people of God three days to gather the treasure that was left for them by the enemy of God. Think about it. Treasures and valuables of such quantities, it took three days to get it all.

We continue to bless the Lord because we are joyful in our restoration! We make a choice to not forget what God has done. We choose to bless the Lord, and we choose to bless Him with a joyful spirit for the restoration in our lives.

Number three. You celebrate! Remember that I told you shouting means to *celebrate our God and His victory.* So after the victory, continue to shout and to celebrate.

Verse 28 tells us, "So they came to Jerusalem, with stringed instruments and harps and trumpets, to the House of the Lord." Can you feel the excitement of that congregation as they entered the temple? Harps being strummed, stringed instruments of all kinds making melody, trumpets sounding a call to worship. No wonder the Psalmist said in Psalm 20:5, "May we shout for joy when we hear of Your victory." Psalm 5:11 says, "I shout for joy because He defends me."

I told you in the eleventh chapter about the word halal. Halal is used more than any other Hebrew word to define praise. It means *to shine, to boast, to celebrate.* I love the excitement at the core of this word. When we say hallelujah, we are celebrating God. Hallelujah implies we are to shine for God in our praise to Him. We should continually, celebrate His goodness in our lives. We should come before Him like little children, with no inhibitions, and celebrate the victory He has won for us. God loves exuberant praise. Understand the value of living a life of celebration and joy. It pleases our Father. After the victory, continue to shout and celebrate!

Number four. You enter into His rest. Verse 30 says, "Then the realm of Jehoshaphat was quiet, for his God gave him rest all around."

Psalm 37:7 says, "Rest in the Lord." When you are not living in the rest of God, you will always revert back to your own abilities and talents.

When I got saved, I tried to help God out. I thought my background as a boxer, a football player, and a professional model would impress people and get them to listen to me. I had a plan, and was working it. And you know, God backed off and let me do just that, work *my* plan. I would go in and speak to high school students, get them laughing and enjoying themselves, but I could never change their lives.

After a couple of years I fell on my knees one day and prayed, "Lord, I don't see people getting saved. No one is being healed. I need Your help."

Then the Lord said, "Are you ready to do it My way?" He directed me to fast. One of the greatest things the Lord spoke to me during the fast was, "Billy, get out of the way." I realized that day God did not need my testimony. I needed His. At the moment I entered His rest, I never again had to prove anything.

Jesus told us in Matthew 11:28-29, "Come to Me, all you who labor and are heavy laden, and I will give you rest. Take My yoke upon you and learn from Me, for I am gentle and lowly in heart, and you will find rest for your souls." When the Lord told me to write a book on shout,

I could not see in the natural how this could happen. But I knew the yoke of God was easy, and so I finally said yes, I would do it. The moment I said yes, I entered His rest. The first couple of times I mentioned the project to a congregation, almost half of the money needed for publishing was received.

There is a vast difference in a good idea and a God idea. When God is in it, it becomes easy.

Hebrews 4:9 says, "There remains therefore a rest for the people of God."

My prayer for you is that every day of your life will be spent in the rest of the Lord.

After the wall has fallen down, after the giant has been defeated, after the mountain has been removed, what is left for you to do?

- Continue to bless the Lord
- Live joyful in your restoration
- Celebrate the victory
- Enter into the rest of God

Blessing God, living joyfully in your restoration, celebrating His victory over the enemy, even entering into His rest will be accompanied by passion. God intends for us to be passionate in life. He has given us a boisterous voice to release joy into the atmosphere.

We came into the world with a shout, and when Jesus returns for us, we will leave with a shout! 1 Thessalonians 4:16 says, "For the Lord Himself will descend from heaven with a shout, with the voice of an archangel, and with the trumpet of God. And the dead in Christ will rise first. Then we who are alive and remain shall be caught up together with them in the clouds to meet the Lord in the air."

Our Father is calling His church to begin to *shout unto God with a voice of triumph*. All over the world as people get a revelation of the shout, we are hearing testimonies of healings and deliverances. Let us not just come in with a shout and go out with a shout, but continue to shout in celebration of God's victory. SHOUT!

PERSONAL PRAYER

If you do not know Jesus Christ as your personal Savior or you are not living for Him right now, then say this prayer.

Dear Jesus, forgive me for sinning against You. Come into my heart. I receive You as my Savior and make You the Lord of my life. From this time forward, I will love You and serve You with all of my heart, my soul, my strength, and my mind. In Jesus' name I pray. Amen.

1 John 1:9 says, "If we confess our sins, He is faithful and just to forgive us our sins and to cleanse us from all unrighteousness." Now that is something to shout about!

To request additional copies of this book,
or to schedule a service in your church or area,
please contact Billy.

PHONE:
972-985-4684

WEBSITE:
www.billygibson.org

EMAIL ADDRESS:
billygibsonministries@msn.com

We would like to hear from you.
Please send your comments about this book to us.
Thank you.

ABOUT THE AUTHOR

Billy Gibson is an Evangelist called to a ministry that focuses on bringing hope and healing to the hurting with special emphasis on prayer for the sick. Several years ago, the Lord spoke to Billy and told him to lay his hands on the sick and He would do the work. Since then, God has released many healings and miracles.